Moaning Morris

by

Ginny Adair-Franklin

This book is published by
Grosvenor House Publishing Ltd
Link House
140 The Broadway, Tolworth, Surrey, KT6 7HT.
www.grosvenorhousepublishing.co.uk

A CIP record for this book
is available from the British Library

ISBN 978-1-78623-322-6

For my lovely family
Here, there and everywhere.
I love you x

15% of all royalties from sales of this book
will be donated to Brake in memory of Peter.

Morris was a lovely little tortoise, but goodness me did he moan – a lot! He didn't mean to, he didn't particularly like moaning, he just couldn't stop himself.

When he started moaning about one thing he found himself grumbling and moaning about everything, until everybody stopped listening to him. Then he would continue to moan to himself!

One day, while Morris and his mother were together in the garden he started to moan and complain about his shell. 'I wish I didn't have to drag this heavy shell around with me all the time, I can't even play running races with my friends, by the time I get to the start line the race is already won.'

Morris's mother didn't answer him but he continued to moan anyway, only now he was moaning about the children that looked after them. 'Those children never give me the food that I like best. When I want lettuce they give me tomatoes, when I want strawberries I get lettuce. I never get what I want when I want it. I expect that all the other tortoises in the world are given all the things that they love eating at exactly the right time.'

'Morris,' said his mother sternly, 'a lot of tortoises would be very pleased to have such nice food and such kind, thoughtful children looking after them. Do you know there are some children that would forget, or even worse, just not bother to feed their pets every day? So think about how lucky you are to be so well cared for.

As for your shell, you are a tortoise, tortoises have shells, that's just the way things are Morris. Please stop moaning. Remember, the grass is always greener on the other side of the fence.'

Then, quick as a wink, she popped inside her shell before Morris could utter another moaning word!

Morris waited, just in case his mother popped back out to listen to more of his moaning. While he waited he thought about what she had said about the grass being greener on the other side of the fence. She always said this to him when he was moaning. It really annoyed him and made him feel even moanier. He thought it was such a silly thing to say. Surely grass is the same wherever you are, after all grass is just grass.

Morris waited for a while. Then, when he realised that his mother wasn't coming out to listen to anymore of his moaning, he decided to see if there was anyone else in the garden that he could moan to.

As soon as the other animals in the garden heard him coming, mumbling and moaning, they scarpered. The rabbit and guinea pigs scrambled for the door to their hutch, all at the same time. They got very tangled up in their hurry to get away, but managed to untangle themselves and disappear through the hutch door just before Morris saw them.

The cat curled up even more tightly than usual and pretended to be fast asleep and the blackbird and sparrows flew off to their nests high in the branches of the apple tree. 'Huh!' Grumbled Morris, 'so much for my friends.'

Slowly, he crawled off through the garden for a sulk, grumbling and moaning as he went.

When Morris reached the bottom of the garden he stopped and looked at the fence. Suddenly he had a great idea! He would climb the fence and take a look over the top just to see if his mother could possibly be right, that grass was greener on the other side.

Slowly and carefully the little tortoise started to climb the pile of broken pots and bricks that had been left against the fence. It wasn't easy to climb because of the heavy shell on his back, but, Morris was determined. So although it was a struggle, he carried on climbing until he reached the top.

He had to stretch his neck as far as he could to see over the top of the fence. 'Just as I expected, the grass looks exactly the same on both sides,' he muttered gleefully.

Morris wanted to get back to his mother as quickly as possible, he couldn't wait to tell her that she had been wrong about the grass, it was the same on both sides.

As Morris started to climb down the fence something unfortunate happened, he caught his shell on a nail!

Morris wiggled and tugged trying to free himself from the nail, but his shell wouldn't budge. He tugged a little harder, but still he was stuck fast. Forgetting that he was at the top of the fence, he gave a great big bad-tempered tug. Well! The shell didn't move off the nail, but Morris moved out of his shell! He shot out at such a speed that he hit the ground with a hard thump.

For a moment he was not sure what had happened. He lay on the grass with his eyes tightly closed. The grass felt strange against his grey, wrinkly skin - of course he had never felt anything but his hard shell before.

Slowly he opened one eye, then the other, he looked around, he could not believe it - he was on the other side of the fence! 'Wow! I'm out in the wide world,' he whispered.

Morris felt very excited but he also felt a little frightened, he had never been out of his garden before, let alone being out in the world. Nor had he left his shell before, in fact he hadn't known that he could leave his shell!

Morris decided that instead of making his way back up and over the fence straight away he would explore the wide world. He set off along the grassy footpath.

Without his heavy shell he was able to walk very fast, then to his delight he discovered that he could run!

Morris ran and ran until he could run no more, then he collapsed in a very happy heap in the lovely cool grass. He lay with the warm sun shining down on him, he felt so happy and content he soon fell into a deep sleep.

Two children were walking along the footpath when they spotted a strange little creature lying in the grass. They couldn't quite make out what the strange creature was at first, because of course they had never seen a tortoise without its shell before.

'Poor little thing,' said one of the children. 'It's a tortoise and it's lost its shell. We better rescue it.' 'Yes, we'll take it home and look after it,' answered the other child, as they quickly stooped down to pick Morris up.

Morris had been woken by the children speaking, but he had kept his eyes closed as he listened to them.

'Oh no,' he said to himself, 'I don't want to be rescued. I want to explore the wide world.' With a silent sigh he resigned himself to his rescue.

Then he remembered that he could run. So, as the children stooped to pick him up he sprang into the air and ran away as fast as his little legs would carry him!

The children were so surprised by Morris suddenly leaping from the ground that they both fell over backwards and stayed sprawled on the grass where they landed, with their mouths and eyes wide open in astonishment!

When Morris thought that he was far enough away from the children he pushed his way through a hedge into a field. He ran to the far side and hid behind a clump of weeds.

Morris laughed quietly, he was very pleased that he had avoided the rescue attempt and was going to be able to continue with his adventure. Morris knew he was going to have to be careful to make sure he was not seen again, as next time he may not be so lucky.

The sun had started to go down and the air was beginning to feel chilly. Morris watched birds as they flew to their nests to roost for the night.

He had felt so free and happy that afternoon that he hadn't given a single thought to where he was going to sleep now that he didn't have his shell – the same shell that he had moaned about so many times!

He also hadn't given a thought to what he was going to eat for his supper now that the children, he had constantly moaned about, were not going to be leaving food out for him.

Morris was missing his mother. He felt cold, sad and lonely, but he was determined that he was not going to moan. He gathered a few nettle leaves and began to eat, they tasted horrible, but they were better than nothing - if only just!

Morris knew he could not stay in the clump of weeds all night. Without his shell he was in danger. A dog, a fox, or some other creature might find him and have him for supper! So, although it had started to get dark, he knew he would have to find a safe warm place to shelter.

As he looked around the field he spotted a little shed in the far corner of the neighbouring field.

The shed looked a little bit like the tortoise shed he lived in back in his own garden only slightly bigger. 'I think that would be perfect. It looks like a safe place for me to rest,' he whispered to himself, 'then I can continue my adventure tomorrow.'

Quickly and quietly, Morris made his way towards the shed. When he reached it, he found there was a trough close by with a few scraps of food left in it. Morris picked out some bits of apple and tomato, he munched on them hungrily.

When he had eaten he looked closely at the shed. There was a little gap at the bottom of the door which he just managed to squeeze through. It was too dark inside the shed for Morris to see anything clearly, but it felt warm and cosy.

Slowly and carefully Morris edged his way around the wall until he found a big pile of warm dry straw, he lay down on the straw and was asleep almost immediately.

The next morning Morris was suddenly woken by a terrible commotion. Huge feathery monsters were leaping and flapping all about the shed, whilst at the same time making deafeningly loud clucking noises!

Morris scrabbled to his feet, slipping and sliding in his hurry to escape these terrible monsters. He couldn't make his way to the small door, which had been pushed open on the other side of the shed, causing the commotion to start, without getting caught up in the middle of them.

Although he was shocked and frightened Morris crouched down in a corner, kept his eyes tightly shut and hoped that the monsters would not spot him! As quickly as the hullabaloo had started it calmed down.

The huge clucking monsters made their way, noisily, out of the shed door. Morris waited for a short time, just to be sure there were no monsters left in the shed.

Quickly, he made his way to the door, stopped, took a deep breath then slowly popped his head out to make sure the monsters were gone.

He got a complete surprise! The monsters were not monsters at all, they were big brown chickens!! He had not known it but he had spent the night in a hen house. Morris chuckled to himself, 'How silly am I? Frightened of chickens indeed.'

Morris made his way back across the fields and back through the hedge onto the footpath. He skipped along humming a little tune to himself. Before long, he was at the end of the footpath where it joined a busy road. There were lots of cars speeding along the road.

Morris didn't like it here, he just knew this was a very dangerous place to be. He crouched down amongst some weeds by the curb and waited for a long gap in the traffic.

As soon as he had the chance Morris crossed the road quickly and very, very, carefully.

When he was at the other side of the road Morris saw a gate leading into a garden. He thought that it would be much safer to go through the gate than to continue along the side of the road.

Luckily there was enough space under the gate for him to easily crawl underneath.

Morris was wary after his fright with the chickens, so he was careful to take a peep under the gate before he went into the garden. He wanted to be certain there would be no scary surprises waiting for him! The garden looked clear of any scariness.

It was a lovely garden with lots of colourful flowers, lots of leafy trees, a beautiful green lawn and best of all a very large vegetable patch.

Morris ran across the lawn and dived into the wonderful vegetable patch, greedily scoffing and gobbling as much lettuce, cabbage, tomatoes and strawberries as he could. He was a very hungry tortoise after his busy morning.

Morris ate all he could, his tummy was stuffed and very, very round! 'Mmm,' He said to himself happily, 'I would like to explore this lovely garden. But, first I must make sure I find somewhere safe and warm to sleep tonight.' Then he chuckled, 'Preferably somewhere there are no scary chickens!'

He looked around and spotted the perfect place. Almost hidden amongst the trees at the bottom of the garden was a huge pile of wood, sticks and dead leaves. Morris was sure there could be nothing hiding in the pile, but he went over to check just to be sure.

The pile of wood and sticks was just the right place to spend the night, and he could also look forward to an enormous breakfast at the vegetable patch!

Now that he had sorted out his sleeping place, Morris spent the rest of the day without a single care, running and playing on the lawn and exploring amongst the flowerbeds. He was so busy playing and having fun he didn't notice a man pushing a wheelbarrow full of more garden rubbish towards the pile of sticks, adding to the already huge pile.

As night began to fall Morris made his way to his sleeping place. He had to push, and squeeze and wriggle to get to the centre of the pile.

He moved a few sharp sticks and prickly brambles around to make a bed, and then he spread a thick layer of dried leaves over the top. After a little work he had a comfortable place to sleep.

The little bed was nice, but it was not as cosy and snug as his well-fitting shell. Morris tossed and turned, but he just couldn't sleep. He had been so busy during the day that he hadn't given a thought to his mother, but now, as he lay all alone in the dark, he realised that he was missing her.

He decided that maybe he had had enough of exploring the wide world, early tomorrow morning he would go back to his mother and to his heavy shell.

Suddenly it occurred to him that as he had been having such a lovely time doing his exploring and running about he hadn't taken any notice of which way he had come, he had no idea of which way he should go to get home - he was lost!

Morris felt very sad, he was sure he would never see his mother again. He started to cry and eventually he cried himself to sleep.

Morris had no way of knowing it, but the pile of sticks and garden rubbish that he had thought a perfect sleeping place was actually a bonfire, and he was in the middle of it!

The man who had made the bonfire had gone home for his tea earlier and now that it was dark he was on his way back to the bonfire to light it. Morris was sound asleep.

As he slept he felt himself getting hotter and hotter. Luckily he woke, he lay still for a moment as he listened to a strange crackling sound.

Then he smelt a strange smoky smell. Suddenly Morris realised what was happening. 'Oh No,' he shouted, 'I'M IN A FIRE!!!'

Morris jumped to his feet and tried to push and shove his way through the sticks, he was panicking and as he pushed his way through the twigs and brambles, his wrinkly skin kept getting caught.

The fire was getting closer to him, he kept pushing on and on, and then suddenly he tumbled out of the sticks onto the grass.

Morris picked himself up and ran to the safety of a flowerbed. He flung himself to the ground, where he lay in the dark on the cold damp earth and cried and cried and cried until he was exhausted. He'd had enough of this adventure all he wanted to do was go home.

Morris was so upset he hadn't seen a big black dog running up to him. The dog looked at Morris, then he started growling and barking fiercely. Morris was silent at once, he tried to scramble away under the flowers, but before he could move very far the big black dog put his paw on Morris's back. Morris couldn't move! The dog had stopped barking and was sniffing at Morris.

'What's your name?' asked the dog in a very gruff, unfriendly way. 'M-M-M-Morris,' stuttered poor Morris. 'What are you then? I've never seen a creature like you before,' continued the dog. I-I-I-I'm a tortoise,' Morris replied in a small frightened voice.

He wanted to ask the dog to take his paw off his back, but he wasn't that brave.

The dog laughed and laughed. 'You silly thing, you can't be a tortoise, you haven't got a shell.'

Then he started laughing again. The dog laughed so much and so hard that he had big round tears running down his cheeks, and he was rolling around on the ground with his paws clutching his tummy.

Morris was getting extremely angry, and this made him forget that he was scared.

'You are a very rude, bad mannered dog to laugh at me. I AM a tortoise but I haven't got my shell on my back.'

Morris tried very hard not to cry again in front of the horrible dog but he could not stop himself.

The dog began to feel sorry for the poor little creature.

'I'm sorry I laughed,' the dog said, sounding a little kinder. 'What happened to your shell?'

Morris told the dog of all his adventures starting with the fence and the nail. He explained how he had caught his shell and had shot out of it, how he was lost, how he was frightened by the chickens, how he had escaped the raging fire, how he was missing his mother and his fear that he would never find his way back to her.

The dog wanted to help poor Morris. 'Jump up on my back and I'll try to help you find your mother.' Morris climbed up onto the dog's shoulder and held on tightly to the dog's collar.

With Morris holding on, the dog made his way out of the garden and across the dangerous road. He continued up the footpath alongside the field where Morris had encountered the chickens.

Then after looking over two or three wrong fences they eventually found the right one.

The dog helped Morris onto the fence. Then, before Morris could thank him, the dog ran off.

Morris climbed down the fence taking great care to avoid the troublesome nail. He searched around beneath the bushes until he found his shell.

Quickly, and with a big joyful sigh, Morris popped inside. His heavy shell felt wonderful, now all he wanted to do was see his mother.

Morris crawled across the garden through the wet dewy grass as fast as he could, which of course as he was now back in his heavy shell, was not very fast!

He was soaking wet but he didn't mind one bit. Morris was in such a hurry to see his mother he almost fell into the little tortoise shed.

He could hear her softly snoring inside her shell. How he had missed that comforting sound.

He tapped very gently on her shell. Sleepily she popped her head out. When she saw Morris she wept with joy. She hugged him so tightly he could hardly breathe.

Morris told his mother that he now understood what she had meant about 'The grass being greener on the other side of the fence.'

He had taken for granted his good life and now realised that all the things that he moaned about were the things he loved about his life.

He told her that he would never ever moan ever again.

Morris's mother smiled at her boy, she knew that he meant it – he would never moan about anything ever again – well not for a week or two anyway!!!

Lightning Source UK Ltd.
Milton Keynes UK
UKHW050300051218
333465UK00006B/151/P